Inspired Nugg

Okay, Okay, I Hear You!

Larnelle Scott

Copyright © 2018 Larnelle Scott

All rights reserved. No portion of this book may be reproduced, stored in a retrieval system, or transmitted in any form or by any means, without the prior written permission of the author.

Interior design, graphics and cover by Allysen Kerr of Antebellum Design Co.

Literary consulting services and editing provided by Clara Rose of RoseDale Communications. Published by RoseDale Publishing, an imprint of RoseDale Communications, Inc.

ISBN: 978-0-9975120-1-4

Dedication

Mama G - I know you're walking around heaven telling everyone that your daughter wrote a book! Thank you for never being shy about letting others know how proud you were of me.

Daddy - You were a man of few words, but you made sure I knew you were crazy about your "Baby Girl". Thank you for that!

Gene, Rhesa & Rudy – You don't know it, but you helped me to <u>hear</u> what He was saying, without which this book would not exist… THANK YOU. I love you dearly!

Table of Contents

Dedication iii

Preface 1

Acknowledgements 3

Introduction 5

One: *I've Got You* 9

Two: *Chill Out* 33

Three: *Quit Fighting... Let Me Have It* 51

Four: *Listen Up* 67

Five: *Stop It* 113

Six: *You've Got This* 129

Seven: *It's Okay... I Promise* 161

Eight: *Love You XOXO* 183

Bibliography 199

About the Author 201

Preface

Dear Reader,

This book is designed to be a launching pad from which you can "blast off" into a new realm of relationship with the Father. It is my hope that you will _hear_ and experience an intimacy with God in a fresh new way. And when you do, feel free to utilize the "call-out" boxes on each page to write down the special "somethings" that you feel He is saying specifically to you.

The scripture reference supports the message He gave to me at that point in time. Please note, at first glance, it may not be evident to you what the connection is between the scripture reference and what He said. When this occurs, let this experience be a motivation to talk to God about it.

In each chapter, there is at least one message that doesn't have a scripture associated with it. You are encouraged to ask God to lead you to a scripture that connects what He's saying to you and write it down on that page.

Throughout the book I have indicated Bible versions that, for me, seemed to really drive home the message. Remember, this book is _your_ launching pad. Use it however you are led on any given day. Whatever happens will reflect your special connection with the Father.

Even though a few of the messages include references to my being female, the message itself is not gender specific. All the tenets of a parent-child love relationship can be found throughout the pages of this literary work: Love & Affection, Assurance, Rest, Trust, Direction, Correction, Encouragement and Comfort.

I am excited about the out-of-this-world experience you will have with the Father.

Jarnell

Acknowledgements

To my Jē Jē,

YOU are my RIDE OR DIE.

I Love You!

Introduction

In December 2016, as I customarily do every year, I went about looking for a yearly devotional that I could use to guide my daily quiet times in the coming year.

After flipping through the pages of *Jesus Calling – Enjoying Peace in His Presence* by Sarah Young, I decided that this was the devotional for me. I've had several devotionals over the years, in which I would make notes on things I learned. However, on January 1, 2017, I was reading the Introduction to the *Jesus Calling* devotional, and the author mentioned that she decided to '*listen with pen in hand, writing down whatever*' she *heard* in her mind.

I, then, heard the Lord tell me to hold my pen as I read and meditate on the daily excerpts because He just may have something to say to me, in particular.

So as a matter of practice, I held the <u>very same pen</u> each day as I read the devotional, all year long, ready to write whatever I heard HIM say. I would also write whatever I wanted to say to HIM. HE began to share (what I call *nuggets*) with me... tidbits of wisdom and valuable spiritual directions, insights and statements. After just a few days of doing so, He spoke to my inner being and told me that I was to make these *nuggets* available to others by putting them in print.

So, I purchased a spiral ring of index cards and began writing them down. Did HE give me a *nugget* each day? No, HE didn't. But did HE give me the *nuggets* HE desired? Absolutely!!

Several years prior, I made a practice of writing actual scriptures on another spiral ring of index cards during my quiet time with Him, scriptures that seemed to speak directly to me and my situation.

In January 2018, once I had completed reading through the *Jesus Calling* devotional, I was led to add a scripture reference to each *nugget*.

The Lord impressed upon my spirit that there were scriptures on this initial spiral ring of index cards that provided a scriptural basis for the *nuggets* He had shared with me.

So, I proceeded to read each *nugget* and prayerfully followed His leading on which of the scriptures He would have me use to highlight each *nugget*. What an experience... scriptures that had spoken to my spirit years prior, were now supporting the *nuggets* God had shared with me throughout 2017. Jesus Christ the same yesterday, today and forever!

What I found is that He didn't just want me to hear what He was saying but he wanted me to hear and do... to respond to what I *heard* by *doing* exactly what He said. He wanted me to Shama (the Hebrew word for hear/listen with the intent to obey). I found that when I did Shama, I found courage, fortitude and solace to deal with the daily issues of life.

It is my prayer that you, too, will find the strength to "do" after reading some of these *nuggets*. As you read these *nuggets* take a moment to listen for what the Father is saying to you... specifically. And, when you find a *nugget* without a scripture reference, that is your opportunity to make it personal by finding and writing down the scripture HE gives you for that *nugget* at that particular time. SHAMA.

As of this writing, I've not met Sarah Young. However, I want to extend my heartfelt appreciation to you, Ms. Young, for allowing the Lord to use you to author the *Jesus Calling* devotional. Because you did, I did. It was the vehicle that propelled me into this unforeseen work. Thank You!!

CHAPTER ONE: ASSURANCE

I've Got You!

"YES."

2 Corinthians 1:20 NIV

I've Got You!

"Wherever you are, I am there... FOREVER, whatever you need, I am that FOREVER."

Psalm 46:5

I've Got You!

"When you run to ME for protection, it activates MY shield."

Psalm 37:40 NIV

I've Got You!

"Be still, MY child, I got you."

Jeremiah 23:29 AMP

I've Got You!

"Troubles you will encounter, that's a part of life; but I have mastered all trouble... and that's a part of LIFE (Me)."

John 16:33 AMP

I've Got You!

"Don't look in fear or unwanted expectation about what's coming. Stay close to Me… look at Me… and by the time it's time to face that thing, it will seem miniscule and passing through it will almost seem effortless. I got this."

2 Chronicles 20:12 AMP

I've Got You!

"I will make you surefooted in dangerous, difficult places."

Psalm 41:11

I've Got You!

"Just like I did for the children of Israel..."

Psalm 115:14

I've Got You!

"I got you… just hold on."

Psalm 84:11

I've Got You!

"And I mean NO-thing."

Jeremiah 32:17

I've Got You!

"I am Immanuel…
God with you. I got you."

Isaiah 51:16 NIV

I've Got You!

"I am with you all the way."

Genesis 28:15 NIV

I've Got You!

"I'm there."

Zechariah 2:5

I've Got You!

"I got you. Jump!"

Isaiah 54:4 NIV

I've Got You!

"I'm doing this... it's Me.

Look for my hand in everything."

1 Kings 12:24 NIV

I've Got You!

"I got you. Everything is going to be alright."

Psalm 37:39-40

I've Got You!

"... and I mean that."

Mark 11:22, 24

I've Got You!

"Yes, I do."

Psalm 119:49

I've Got You!

"I certainly am."

Psalm 46:1-2

I've Got You!

"I got this. As you say, I'm your 'Ride or Die'."

Psalm 102:13 NIV

I've Got You!

"Yep."

I've Got You!

"Trust Me."

CHAPTER TWO: REST

Chill Out

Chill Out

"Relax... float."

Jeremiah 29:11 NIV

Chill Out

"Let go of you and rest in Me… float in Me. That way you will move with the current of My doings."

Isaiah 48:17 NIV

Chill Out

"Believe... Rest... Receive."

Hebrews 4:3 AMP

Chill Out

"Sit still and _know_."

Isaiah 46:9-10 NIV

Chill Out

"Stay with Me, girl, Stay with Me."

John 11:40

Chill Out

"Linger... relax... I got this. Here we go..."

✎ Isaiah 35:4-6 NIV

Chill Out

"Exhale in My Presence."

Isaiah 30:15 AMP

Chill Out

"Let me do it... rest."

1 Kings 8:56

Chill Out

"Return to Me and rest.

That's where your deliverance is."

Jeremiah 33:3

Chill Out

"Lean hard on Me."

Deuteronomy 33:27

Chill Out

"I am doing all the work;

all you have to do is 'Let'."

Zechariah 4:6

Chill Out

"I'll give you glimpses... look at Me."

🖊 Deuteronomy 4:35

Chill Out

"The more you rest,

the more you are able to receive."

Joshua 21:44 NIV

Chill Out

"Rest... in Me." :-)

✎ Exodus 33:14

Chill Out

"Rest, MY child, rest."

CHAPTER THREE: TRUST

Quit Fighting... Let Me Have It

Quit Fighting... Let Me Have It

"When you feel the pressure of MY hand molding you, just say YES."

Luke 1:38

Quit Fighting... Let Me Have It

"When things seem to be falling apart all around you, TRUST ME. When you don't see the desired change in the desired timeframe, TRUST ME. When you're at the threshold of the door of destruction, TRUST ME. I love you. I got you. Don't despair and give in to fleshly thoughts and ways. TRUST ME."

Psalm 84:12 AMP

Quit Fighting... Let Me Have It

"Make a conscious decision to trust Me. Trust Me... on purpose."

Psalm 5:11

Quit Fighting... Let Me Have It

"Practice trusting for the small so that you will be ready to trust Me for the BIG."

1 Thessalonians 5:24 NIV

Quit Fighting... Let Me Have It

"Let ME have it."

Isaiah 22:22 NIV

Quit Fighting... Let Me Have It

"Expend your energy trusting ME."

1 Corinthians 4:20 NIV

Quit Fighting... Let Me Have It

"Let ME do what I do in you."

Isaiah 49:5

Quit Fighting... Let Me Have It

"Don't fight... trust."

Isaiah 12:6

Quit Fighting... Let Me Have It

"Everything I do is BIG!

I can't help it!"

Psalm 103:19 NIV

Quit Fighting... Let Me Have It

"The world says, 'The devil is in the details,' so let Me handle the details... and consequently the devil."

Isaiah 59:19 AMP

Quit Fighting... Let Me Have It

"To walk above your circumstance, the only thing you must see is <u>Me</u>. Once you see the turmoil around you, your faith dissipates, and you begin to sink <u>in</u> that you once walked <u>on</u>."

Habakkuk 3:19 AMP

Quit Fighting... Let Me Have It

"Trust out loud."

Job 22:27-28 AMP

Quit Fighting... Let Me Have It

"Trust ME with ALL."

Acts 27:25 NIV

Quit Fighting... Let Me Have It

"It's ME, I'm all you need. It's ME, It's ME dear (insert your name here)."

CHAPTER FOUR: DIRECTION

Listen Up

Listen Up

"Shhhh."

Habakkuk 2:20

Listen Up

"Wait... First."

1 Samuel 12:16

Listen Up

"Wait to see if what you plan to do is what I plan to do."

Isaiah 11:2-3 AMP

Listen Up

"Don't get off the path. Stay on the path, (insert your name), stay on track."

Proverbs 23:18 NIV

Listen Up

"Stay the course, don't rush it."

Jeremiah 29:14

Listen Up

"When I don't say anything in particular, don't move."

Numbers 22:18

Listen Up

"Free will is My gift to you. Cherish it! Be careful not to abuse this privilege."

Numbers 14:28 NIV

Listen Up

"Flow, Girl, Flow."

Habakkuk 2:2-3

Listen Up

"Become more and more like ME!"

Psalm 51:10

Listen Up

"Don't be lazy in your praying."

Proverbs 18:21

Listen Up

"Don't ignore ME during the day."

2 Chronicles 16:9a

Listen Up

"Just keep looking, (insert your name) keep looking."

Habakkuk 3:2 NIV

Listen Up

"You need to always be listening, always in listening mode."

Isaiah 30:21 AMP

Listen Up

"Stay."

Job 37:5

Listen Up

"Include me in <u>Everything</u>. I care."

Psalm 57:2 AMP

Listen Up

"Just keep doing what you're doing. Don't look back & don't look around. Just keep movin'."

Psalm 18:36 AMP

_____
_____
_____
_____
_____
_____
_____
_____
_____
_____

Listen Up

"Be in learning mode."

Isaiah 28:26 NIV

Listen Up

"Live your best life TODAY. Enjoy the moment."

Psalm 37:25 NIV

Listen Up

"Don't live 'safe'. Live sure."

Daniel 11:32b

Listen Up

"Don't let the circumstance determine your response."

Ecclesiastes 11:4-6 AMP

Listen Up

"Scurrying and hurrying gets you nowhere. Progress is in Me. Slow down."

Exodus 12:36 AMP

Listen Up

"Talk to Me... about everything."

    James 5:16 NIV

Listen Up

"Never take a break from me - I'm all you got."

Psalm 78:41-42

Listen Up

"Don't do what comes naturally; do what comes supernaturally."

Psalm 18:29 AMP

Listen Up

"Stop first to remember... then pray. This will help stir up your faith."

1 Samuel 7:12 NIV

Listen Up

"Depend on me. I love the needy."

John 11:40 AMP

Listen Up

"Stop trying to figure out 'how' it's working together for good. Just know that it is and thank ME for it."

Luke 1:45 NIV

Listen Up

"Expect ME... not someone or something else. Expect ME and ME alone."

Deuteronomy 32:4

Listen Up

"Always seek to see the BIGGER picture, My child. Ask Me... I created the picture. I am the Artiste." :-)

Job 28:10b AMP

Listen Up

"AKA... Believe."

✎ Exodus 14:13

Listen Up

"My grace is sufficient for thee. Use the faith I'VE given you to propel you into MY grace."

Romans 5:2

Listen Up

"Live in the here and now."

Matthew 6:34 AMP

Listen Up

*"Keep it moving.
Don't let trouble stagnate you."*

Deuteronomy 2:31 AMP

Listen Up

"Just love, (insert your name), just love."

✒ Ecclesiastes 7:9

_____
_____
_____
_____
_____
_____
_____
_____
_____

Listen Up

"Just stay still."

Deuteronomy 28:7 AMP

Listen Up

"Talk Trust, it will help you live Trust."

Psalm 118:17 NIV

Listen Up

"Keep reading..."

Listen Up

"At every period, comma, semicolon - say 'Thank You'."

Listen Up

"Just do that to feel the closeness of My presence."

Listen Up

"'Be a kid' in My presence."

Listen Up

"Resting requires dwelling. In order to rest, you must first dwell."

Listen Up

*"If it's Me... Yield.
If it's the devil... Resist & Rebuke."*

Listen Up

"Be close, very close to ME, but never forget WHO I am."

CHAPTER FIVE: CORRECTION

Stop It

Stop It

"You don't run things... I do."

Psalm 89:8-9 NIV

Stop It

"Remember... I'm the Fixer (not you)."

Zephaniah 3:19a AMP

Stop It

"Do you hear Me? I got this!"

Deuteronomy 8:18 NIV

Stop It

"Cut it out!"

Ephesians 4:32 AMP

Stop It

"Don't join the 'Woe is me' club."

Psalm 91:15

Stop It

"Because you don't really know Me."

✏️ Philippians 3:10 AMP

_____
_____
_____
_____
_____
_____
_____
_____
_____
_____
_____

Stop It

"Don't be flaky."

Psalm 51:10

Stop It

"You must do this thing MY way."

Isaiah 50:7

Stop It

"Then do what I say."

Nehemiah 4:14b NIV

Stop It

"You think too much."

Isaiah 50:2 AMP

Stop It

"It's not about what you are able to do, but what I'M permitting you to do."

2 Corinthians 9:8 AMP

Stop It

*"Quit pining over what was.
Find MY will & way in what's now."*

Isaiah 43:18-19 NIV

Stop It

"*So, stop trying.*"

Proverbs 10:22 AMP

Stop It

"I'm not playing hide-and-seek with you. I'm in clear view if you just look."

CHAPTER SIX: ENCOURAGEMENT

You've Got This!

You've Got This!

"Man will, but I won't, Man won't but I will."

Isaiah 44:2-3 NIV

You've Got This!

"Even when you can't, I can & will, if you let Me."

Habakkuk 1:5 NIV

You've Got This!

"Weakness or worry? I'm using that too!"

2 Corinthians 12:9

You've Got This!

"Don't get hung up on your hang-ups."

Ephesians 2:10 NIV

You've Got This!

"I made you... remember?"

Jeremiah 32:27

You've Got This!

"Even when others aren't."

Hebrews 10:23

You've Got This!

"Enjoy Now... what you think, or hope is coming may never arrive!"

Matthew 6:34 AMP

You've Got This!

"Absolutely!"

Joshua 21:45 AMP

You've Got This!

"Take a look at MY life on earth and among men. I was misunderstood, talked about, betrayed, abandoned and eventually killed. So, don't get disheartened. Hang in there. I got you, Baby Girl, I got you!"

Acts 20:24 AMP

You've Got This!

*"It's alright to be human because... you are!
I made you that way, remember?"*

Romans 8:11 NIV

You've Got This!

"It's up to you."

Deuteronomy 9:1

You've Got This!

"You can, you have every right to, but you don't... that's meekness."

Micah 6:8 AMP

You've Got This!

"That's right, I told you to do that."

✎ Habakkuk 2:2-3 AMP

You've Got This!

"Try it, you'll like it!"

🖊️ 1 Samuel 30:8

You've Got This!

"No limits!"

Ephesians 3:20

You've Got This!

"Walking with ME is an adventure... an experience. Enjoy!"

Deuteronomy 1:11 AMP

You've Got This!

"Work with Me. There's a definite method to this seeming madness."

Isaiah 49:23

You've Got This!

"Keep your eyes on ME! If you do, you too will be able to walk on water."

Psalm 18:32-33 AMP

You've Got This!

"Transformation hurts...
but it's oh so necessary."

Ecclesiastes 7:8

You've Got This!

"I had to look beyond the cross in order to go to, and through, the cross."

1 John 4:17

You've Got This!

*"I can handle it,
even when others don't understand.
So, don't worry about your weaknesses."*

Isaiah 49:25

You've Got This!

"Do it (insert your name)."

Joshua 18:3

You've Got This!

"Stay close."

Proverbs 4:20-22 NIV

You've Got This!

"You are on the right path. Slow down and enjoy ME!"

✎ Psalm 16:11 NIV

You've Got This!

"Enjoy the ride." :-)

Deuteronomy 8:7-9 NIV

You've Got This!

"I'm your very best bet. As a matter of fact, I'm not a bet/gamble at all. I'm your Sure Thing!"

Isaiah 41:13 NIV

You've Got This!

"Cuz you will be able to love like I love... condition free."

You've Got This!

"Just like a sailor finds a fixed point on the shoreline to determine how he's moving, make ME your fixed focus point and you will be able to see how you are moving along just fine."

You've Got This!

"Say MY name, say MY name...
it helps!"

CHAPTER SEVEN: COMFORT

It's Okay... I Promise

It's Okay... I Promise

"No matter what your circumstances are screaming, I am always there!"

Habakkuk 3:17-18 NIV

It's Okay... I Promise

"This thing is of ME."

Luke 1:49

It's Okay... I Promise

"Don't be shy. Come to me. I'm your Daddy. You have that right!"

1 Chronicles 4:10 NIV

It's Okay... I Promise

*"I already know...
and already love you."*

Hebrews 6:9a

It's Okay... I Promise

"... and I understand you."

Psalm 40:17 AMP

It's Okay... I Promise

"I add to what you lack to make you complete."

Ezekiel 11:19 AMP

It's Okay... I Promise

"I also am your REARGUARD."

Psalm 89:18

It's Okay... I Promise

"You can depend on ME..."

Philippians 4:13

It's Okay... I Promise

"...and you shall not want."

Isaiah 3:10

It's Okay... I Promise

"Settle down now. Everything is OK."

Zephaniah 3:17

It's Okay... I Promise

"*I know where all of the underwater potholes are.*"

Isaiah 45:2 AMP

It's Okay... I Promise

"I am Totality."

Luke 1:37

It's Okay... I Promise

"...and know I have power over everything."

Proverbs 21:1

It's Okay... I Promise

"I will_____. You can fill in the blank. Just know that I will."

Isaiah 65:24

It's Okay... I Promise

"In the midst of darkness, I reign."

Mark 5:36 NIV

It's Okay... I Promise

"I know."

It's Okay... I Promise

"Nothing catches ME by surprise."

It's Okay... I Promise

"My Presence = your peace."

It's Okay... I Promise

"...and I alone."

CHAPTER EIGHT: LOVE & AFFECTION

Love You XOXO

"No matter what you do, I LOVE YOU!"

Isaiah 65:16b AMP

"I really do love you... no holds barred."

Deuteronomy 1:32

Love You XOXO

"Walk with ME & experience heaven."

Exodus 19:5

"Cuz I love you dearly."

Genesis 12:2

"You're welcome. Anytime." :-)

Psalm 116:5 NIV

"I love the intimacy."

Proverbs 8:21 AMP

"Spend time with ME.
It will be worth your while."

Job 22:21

"Enjoy ME."

Proverbs 8:17-21

"Love on ME."

2 Samuel 24:24 AMP

"Tend to ME."

Psalm 103:20 NIV

Love You XOXO

"... I love you too."

"*I love you even when I have to chastise you. I chastise you <u>because</u> I love you.*"

Love You XOXO

"Love you too, Baby Girl...
don't you ever forget it!"

"I love you constantly because you need ME constantly."

Bibliography

Unless otherwise noted, Scripture quotations are taken from the Holy Bible, King James Version (KJV). Copyright © 1611, 1769. Public domain.

THE AMPLIFIED BIBLE (AMP). Copyright © 1954, 1958, 1962, 1964, 1965, 1987 by The Lockman Foundation. All rights reserved.

Used by permission (www.Lockman.org)

New International Version, (NIV). Copyright © 1973, 1978, 1984 by Biblica, Inc.

Used by permission of Zondervan. All rights reserved worldwide. www.zondervan.com.

The 'NIV' and 'New International Version' are trademarks registered in the United States patent and Trademark Office by Biblica, Inc.

About the Author

Larnelle Scott has a history of actively serving in various ministries in the local church (i.e. choir director, musician, usher, finance, church school teacher, church school superintendent, Christian education, executive council, administration). She actively served in Chicago, New York, and Atlanta for many years and continues to do so in Tampa Florida.

During all four years of college, she was active with Campus Crusade for Christ. She has participated in numerous street evangelism and witnessing efforts and was involved in mission efforts in the U.S. and abroad.

HOWEVER, her ministry experience is not what prompted her to write this book. Larnelle writes this book in obedience to the direct instructions she received from the Father. It has been a complete faith journey... one that she never saw coming. She doesn't know "why" she was instructed to write this book, but she is certain about "Who" told her and "what" she was told to do. She is satisfied that HE is satisfied.

Larnelle would love to hear about your experience as you read through the pages of this book...

she can be contacted on her FaceBook page or by email.

https://www.facebook.com/LarnelleScottAuthor

OkayOkayIHearYou@gmail.com

#OkayOkayIHearYou

Made in the USA
Columbia, SC
19 January 2019